THE DECREE OF 610

Gundemar,

King of Visigothic Spain

Translated by: D.P. Curtin

Dalcassian
Publishing
Company

PHILADELPHIA, PA

ISBN: **978-1-960069-71-9** (Paperback)

Library of Congress Control Number:
Author: Curtin, D.P. (1985-)

Front cover image: Rey de los Visigodos (Museo del Prado) Bernardino Montañés
Book design by J.J. Ripplestick

Printed by Ingram Content Group, 1 Ingram Blvd, La Vergne, Tennessee

First printing edition 2020.

Introduction

The specific reigns of the Visigothic kings of Spain are obscured by the cataclysm of the Arab conquest. Unlike that of the Frankish administration, which transitioned from the decentralized and ineffectual Merovingian dynasty to the zenith of Frankish power under the Carolingians, the Spanish nations had no such continuity. Its institutions were cut down rather abruptly in 717 AD when the armies of the Moors marched north to subdue the nation for the next eight centuries.

One of the few institutions to largely survive the cataclysm, was that of the Spanish Catholic church. A royalist revival would eventual lead the alleged 'Reconquista' under the banners of various Spanish crowns, but the church was (and remains) the foundation of the Spanish nation. Some of the few surviving artifacts from Visigothic rule are ecclesiastical or relate to the Catholic church's present in post-Roman Spain. To this point, church documents grant some rare insights into the royal court that would otherwise be unknown because of the loss of Visigothic royal authority. Collectively there are various documents relating the Synods at Toledo, that helped former the embryonic Spanish church as it struggled to survive the transition of power. However, these documents only have a passive relationship to the political institution of the Spanish crown. They speak more to the confused relationship between bishops and the struggle against the Arian heresy then they do about the Spanish constitution.

This document is one of the rare royal documents of the period which give voice to a Visigothic king, or perhaps his ghost writer, and allows us to see the nature to the relationship of the Spanish crown to the Catholic church. This relationship is perhaps as pertinent to the 7th century as it is today, as both institutions remain highly influential. Moreover, we are also given a brief insight into Byzantine-Spanish relations in this period, something that is not heavily discussed by chroniclers of the period. Here the Spanish king feels that Byzantine-African bishops are challenging his supremacy over the church and seeks to re-assert the role of the king over the bishops in his realm.

Curiously, the Eastern Roman Emperor is not mentioned, and is omission appears pregnant with meaning. It seems unlikely that the Spanish king would actively seek out the potential wrath of the Empire, and so the wording of the decree if cautiously political, making statements based upon ecclesiastical precedent, then that utilizing the brute force commonly associated with western barbarians in the Greek imagination.

D.P. Curtin
February 21, 2020
Glen Mills, PA

King Flavius[1] Gundemarus to our venerable Fathers, the Carthaginian priests[2]:

Although the care of our kingdom seems to be the most prompt in arranging and governing the affairs of the human race, yet our majesty is most gloriously decorated with the fame of virtues, when those things which belong to the order of divinity and religion are arranged with equity in the straightest courses. Knowing, therefore, that on account of this, our piety, would not only obtain the long-term title of temporal dominion, but also the eternal glory of merit.

---

[1] Here the Visigothic king is given an old Roman first name, this appears as a small fragment of Roman culture a century and a half after the Western Empire had collapsed.
[2] The exact nature of the controversy is not known, but it appears to be a jurisdictional issue with the Catholic Byzantine bishops.

For some in the ecclesiastical disciplines, against the authority of the canons, through the delays of previous times, took license for usurping the past prince[3]. So that some of the bishops of the province of Carthage did not respect, against the opinion of the canonical authority, sporadically and freely, against the power of the archbishop church, through certain fraternities and conspiracies, all unexplored lives were advanced to the episcopal office, and to despise this very dignity of the aforesaid church exalted on the throne of our empire. This disturbed the truth of the ecclesiastical order, and abused the authority of its seat, which the ancient opinion of the canons declared. We by no means allowed ourselves to be done beyond this method until forever, but we showed the primacy of honor, according to the ancient authority of the synodal council, for all the churches of the province of Carthage to have a bishop of the seat of the church of Toletana[4]. Among his co-bishops, he was preeminent in both honor and dignity.

According to which the ancient tradition of the canons sanctioned the archbishops in each province, and the ancient authority permitted. We do not allow the same Carthaginian province to be divided under the rule of two archbishops against the decrees of the Fathers, whereby a variety of schisms arise, by which faith is subverted and unity is divided. This very seat[5], as has been said, the ancient seat of his name, and of our worship of the empire, so that the entire province may be filled with the dignity of the church and may be preeminent in power.

---

[3] That being Witteric, King of Goths, although regal supremacy of the church had been a point of the Third Synod of Toledo some decades before as well.
[4] That is Toledo, here rendered closer to the original Latin *Toletum*.
[5] That is the *Cathedra* of the bishop of Toledo, which was allegedly founded by Eugenius, a disciple of St. Dionysius the Areopagite, a disciple of St. Paul

And that which was already noted long ago in the general synod of the council of Toletane by the venerable bishop Euphemius[6], with the signature of his hand, that Toletane was the seat of the metropolis of the province of Carpetania[7]. We correct the same opinion born of ignorance. Knowing beyond a doubt that the region of Carpetania is not a province, but a part of the province of Carthage[8], according to which the ancient records of events declare. For this reason, because it is one and the same province, we decree that, as Baetica, Lusitania, or the province of Tarracon, or the rest belonging to the governments of our kingdom, according to the ancient decrees of the Fathers.

And that each one is known to have its own archbishop, just as the province of Carthage has one and the same person, whom the ancient synodal authority declares, and who is venerated as the primate, and who among all the co-provincials honors the highest religious status. Let nothing be done with the same contempt, such as the proud presumption of the arrogant priests has hitherto tempted.

---

[6] The 23rd bishop of Toledo

[7] This is an older Latin term for the region, being derived from the pre-Roman tribes in the region known as the Carpentani. Its distinctive identity was maintained into the Visigothic period, but vanished following the Arab conquest.

[8] The question at hand is relating to the jurisdictional limits of the Archbishop of Carthage. Following the collapse of the Western Roman state, full jurisdiction was held by the Visigothic bishops. However, with the conquests of the Emperor Justinian I, Imperial jurisdiction was pushed on the southern coast of Spain through its Exarchate in Carthage.

Of course, by this edict of our authority, we give the tenor of manners and living, and the law of religion, or of innocence. Nor afterwards do we suffer the like to be done with inordinate license from the bishops, but through our clemency, in view of past negligence, in view of piety, we both grant pardon and grant the help of indulgence. While it is a great fault that they have transgressed hitherto, yet a greater and inexcusable censure will hold them liable to those who have attempted to violate this decree of ours, coming from the authority of the ancient Fathers, by reckless daring. Every one of the Carthaginian priests of the Church despised him[9]. Without a doubt he will suffer in disobedience both the sentence of ecclesiastical degradation or excommunication, and also the censure of our severity. For we, having disposed such things in the divine Churches, believe faithfully that the kingdom of our empire is so divinely governed by a just king, just as we gold to order in our worship, fired with the zeal of justice, and strive to correct it, and intend to perpetuate it forever.

---

[9] This might be Fortunius, who is noted as one of the last bishops of Carthage, although little is known to him.

LATIN TEXT

Flavius Gundemarus rex venerabilibus Patribus nostris Carthaginensibus sacerdotibus.

Licet regni nostri cura in disponendis atque gubernandis humani generis rebus promptissima esse videatur, tunc tamen majestas nostra maxime gloriosiori decoratur fama virtutum, cum ea quae ad Divinitatis et religionis ordinem pertinent, aequitate rectissimi tramitis disponuntur; scientes ob hoc pietatem nostram non solum diuturnum temporalis imperii consequi titulum, sed etiam aeternorum adipisci gloriam meritorum. Nonnulli enim in disciplinis ecclesiasticis, contra canonum auctoritatem, per moras praecedentium temporum, licentiam sibi de usurpatione praeteriti principis fecerunt: ita ut quidam episcoporum Carthaginensis provinciae non revereantur, contra canonicae auctoritatis sententiam, passim ac libere, contra metropolitanae Ecclesiae potestatem, per quasdam fratrias, et conspirationes, inexploratae vitae omnes episcopali officio provehi, atque hanc ipsam praefatae Ecclesiae dignitatem imperii nostri solio sublimatam contemnere; perturbantes ecclesiastici ordinis veritatem, ejusque sedis auctoritate, quam prisca canonum declarat sententia, abutentes. Quod nos ultra modo usque in perpetuum fieri nequaquam permittimus, sed honorem primatus, juxta antiquam synodalis concilii auctoritatem, per omnes Carthaginensis provinciae ecclesias Toletanae ecclesiae sedis episcopum habere ostendimus: eumque inter suos coepiscopos, tam honoris praecellere dignitate quam nominis; juxta quod de metropolitanis per singulas provincias antiqua canonum traditio sanxit, et auctoritas vetus permisit. Neque eamdem Carthaginensem provinciam in ancipiti duorum metropolitanorum regimine contra Patrum decreta permittimus dividendam, per quod oriatur varietas schismatum, quibus subvertatur fides, et unitas scindatur; sed haec ipsa sedes, sicut praedictum est, antiqua nominis sui, ac nostri cultu imperii, ita et totius provinciae polleat ecclesiae dignitate, et praecelleat potestate.

Illud autem quod jam pridem in generali synodo concilii Toletani a venerabili Euphemio episcopo manus subscriptione notatum est, Carpetaniae provinciae Toletanam esse sedem metropolim, nos ejusdem ignorantiae sententiam corrigimus: scientes procul dubio Carpetaniae regionem non esse provinciam, sed partem Carthaginensis provinciae, juxta quod et antiqua rerum gestarum monumenta declarant. Ob hoc, quia una eademque provincia est, decernimus ut, sicut Baetica, Lusitania, vel Tarraconensis provincia, vel reliquae ad regni nostri regimina pertinentes, secundum antiqua Patrum decreta, singulos noscuntur habere metropolitanos, ita et Carthaginensis provincia unum eumdemque, quem prisca synodalis declarat auctoritas, et veneretur primatem, et inter omnes comprovinciales summum honoret antistitem; neque quidquam contempto eodem ultra fiat, qualia hactenus arrogantium sacerdotum superba tentavit praesumptio. Sane per hoc auctoritatis nostrae edictum, amodo et vivendi damus tenorem, et religionis, vel innocentiae legem; nec ultra postmodum inordinata licentia ab episcopis similia fieri patimur, sed per nostram clementiam praeteritae negligentiae, pietatis intuitu, et veniam damus, et indulgentiae opem concedimus: et dum sit magna culpa hactenus deliquisse, majoris tamen ac inexpiabilis censura tenebit obnoxios, qui hoc nostrum decretum, ex auctoritate priscorum Patrum veniens, temerario ausu violare tentaverint: nec ultra veniam delicti faciemus admissi, adempti, si dehinc honorem ejusdem Ecclesiae quilibet Carthaginiensium sacerdotum contempserit; subiturus procul dubio inobediens tam degradationis, vel excommunicationis ecclesiasticae sententiam, quam etiam nostrae severitatis censuram. Nos enim talia in divinis Ecclesiis disponentes credimus fideliter regnum imperii nostri ita divino gubernaculo regi, sicut et nos cultum ordinis, zelo justitiae accensi, et corrigere studemus, et in perpetuum perseverare disponimus

The Scriptorium Project is the work of a small group of lay people of various apostolic churches who are interested in the preservation, transmission, and translation of the works of the early and medieval church. Our efforts are to make the works of the church fathers accessible to anyone who might have an interest in Christian antiquities and the theological, philosophical, and moral writings that have become the bedrock of Western Civilization.

To-date, our releases have pulled from the Greek, Syriac, Georgian, Latin, Celtic, Ethiopian, and Coptic traditions of Christianity, and have been pulled from sundry local traditions and languages.

Other Titles and Translations by D.P. Curtin:

First Book of Ethiopian Maccabees (2018)
Protoevangelium of James: Greek and English Texts (2019)
Edicts of the Synod of Paris by Chlothar II, King of Franks (2019)
The Life of St. Desiderius by Sisebut, King of Visigoths (2019)
The Synod of Rome by St. Boniface IV of Rome (2019)
Letter to Pope Theodore by Victor of Carthage (2020)
The Decree of 610 by Gundemar, King of Visigoths (2020)
Laws of the Church by Dagobert I, King of Franks (2020)
The Old Nubian Miracle of St. Mena (2021)
About Fifteen Problems by St. Albertus Magnus (2022)
Testament of Some Former Things by John Scotus Eriugena (2022)
The Georgian Synaxarium (2022)
Instructions: Counsel for Novices by St. Ammonas the Hermit (2022)
The Syriac Menologium and Martyrology (2022)
Book on Religious Exercise and Quiet by St. Isaiah the Solitary (2022)
Vision of Theophilus by St. Cyril of Alexandria (2022)
On Fate (De Fato) by St. Albertus Magnus (2023)
Fragments of 'Chronicle' by Hippolytus of Thebes (2023)
Life of the Blessed Theotokos by Epiphanius Monachus (2023)
Syriac Life of John the Baptist by Serapion the Presbyter (2023)
Second Book of Ethiopian Maccabees (2023)